Garter Snakes

Julie Murray

Abdo
EVERYDAY ANIMALS
Kids

abdopublishing.com

Published by Abdo Kids, a division of ABDO, PO Box 398166, Minneapolis, Minnesota 55439.
Copyright © 2016 by Abdo Consulting Group, Inc. International copyrights reserved in all countries.
No part of this book may be reproduced in any form without written permission from the publisher.

Printed in the United States of America, North Mankato, Minnesota.

102015
012016

THIS BOOK CONTAINS
RECYCLED MATERIALS

Photo Credits: iStock, Shutterstock

Production Contributors: Teddy Borth, Jennie Forsberg, Grace Hansen

Design Contributors: Candice Keimig, Dorothy Toth

Library of Congress Control Number: 2015941761
Cataloging-in-Publication Data
Murray, Julie.
 Garter snakes / Julie Murray.
   p. cm. -- (Everyday animals)
ISBN 978-1-68080-115-6 (lib. bdg.)
Includes index.
1. Garter snakes--Juvenile literature.   I. Title.
597.96--dc23
                    2015941761

Table of Contents

Garter Snakes

Garter snakes are reptiles.

They have scales.

4

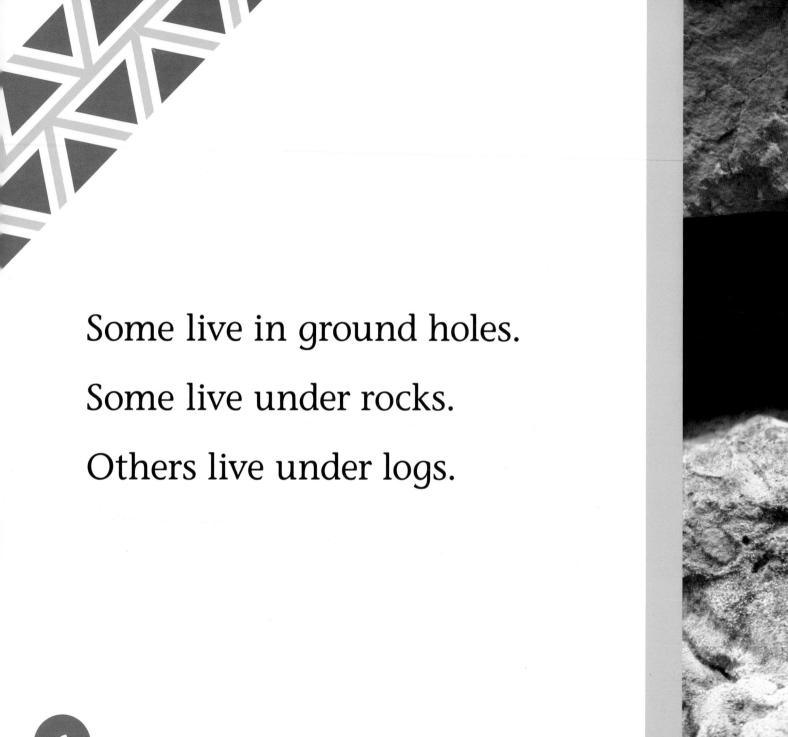

Some live in ground holes.

Some live under rocks.

Others live under logs.

Garter snakes are long.

They are thin.

Many are brown or olive.

Some are black.

Most have stripes.

Garter snakes shed their skin.

New skin grows.

They eat frogs and birds.

They eat mice and ants.

They move side to side.

They make an *S* shape.

They use their tongues to smell.

This helps them find food.

Have you seen a garter snake?

Features of a Garter Snake

Eyes

Tail

Scales

Tongue

Glossary

reptiles
cold blooded animals that often have scales.

scales
thin, flat plates that cover certain animals.

Index

abdokids.com

Use this code to log on to abdokids.com and access crafts, games, videos, and more!

Abdo Kids Code:
EGK1156